Victoria and Albert Museum

Going to Bed

The Arts and Living

Eileen Harris

General editors for the series John Fleming and Hugh Honour

D1638670

London: Her Majesty's Stationery Office

Acknowledgements

My thanks are due, first and foremost, to
Mr. Peter Thornton, keeper of the Department
of Furniture and Woodwork, for his enormous
generosity in providing me with invaluable advice
and information on the history of beds, a subject
on which he is the leading authority. Many other
members of the staff of the Victoria and Albert
Museum have facilitated the progress of my work.
I greatly appreciate their co-operation. Finally, to
Sir Francis Watson, I am indebted for valuable
suggestions and corrections to my manuscript.

With the following exceptions all the objects
illustrated are from the Victoria and Albert
Museum. Figs.2 and 3 British Museum;
Figs.28a,b,c and 37 Science Museum; Fig.30
National Gallery of Canada; Fig.32 Louvre, Paris;
Fig.33 Collection Alan Irvine, London;
Fig.35 Musée Builhet-Christofle, Saint-Denis.

Design by HMSO Graphic Design

ISBN 0 11 290287 1

Contents

1 A Bed Defined   5

2 Fashions in Beds   11

3 Beds for Marriage, Birth and Death   36

4 Caring for The Bed   41

5 Bedrooms   47

6 Bedroom Furniture   56

7 Beds Separate or Shared   61

8 Dressing for Bed   64

9 Getting Up   67

Bibliography   70

Index   72

Preface

This brief book, unlike a voluminous bedcurtain, does not purport to cover its subject completely. It is something of a course-net cast very wide to catch as many of the major points as possible, sacrificing small and often precious details in the process. But I hope its contents are accurate and illuminating, sometimes even edifying. They are intended to conduct the public on a thematic bed-going tour through the whole of the Victoria and Albert Museum.

> In bed we laugh, in bed we cry
> And, born in bed, in bed we die.
>
> (Benserade, translated by Dr. Johnson)

The bed is 'the symbol of life', as de Maupassant said; the measure, as the princess proved by the pea, of the quality of its occupant and all that he can command. It elevates him above the ground where the poor, like animals, lie. It provides him with greater comfort for greater expenditure, boosting self-esteem. In the eyes of the world, it displays his wealth and rank in its dress and decor.

We, in our affluent, egalitarian society, are inclined to take our beds too much for granted. What is this object we use and tend daily, know and cherish so intimately? The answer is not simple. Of all our goods and chattels, the bed is the most complex.

1 A Bed Defined

A bed and a bedstead, although we think of them as one, are, in fact, two distinct objects. A bedstead is an article of furniture, a prop totally subservient to a bed, but not essential to it. A bed is a 'thing to sleep on': a Bedouin's pile of carpets and cushions; a Japanese rice-straw mat *(tatami)* and under-quilt *(shiki-futon)*; our mattress, the 'feather-beddes', quilted and straw ones used by our ancestors. The pad, whatever its composition, is the essence of the bed. Covers, sheets and pillows come next, in order of importance, as providers of warmth and additional comfort. The quantity and quality of these elements vary continually, but their nature and arrangement remain unchanged since antiquity.

A Mattress, by definition the mat, usually of plaited rushes, on which the bed rests, must be considered here, in familiar terms, as the stuffed sack–the tick with stripes of ancient origin–which makes a bed. According to one's means and preference, the stuffing could be anything from straw to swansdown. Wool was the most common choice for those who had one. The feather-bed, or bristle tick, known to but a few Greeks, grew steadily more popular from the Roman period to the early nineteenth century. During this time, comfort was all that was expected of a mattress. Then, as medicine and technology advanced, its hygienic and physiological effects became an increasingly important concern. Now, the mattress has become little more than orthopaedic equipment accompanied, in well appointed American hotels, by coin-operated mechanical massagers. Sleep and comfort have their own prescriptions.

The feather-bed was extremely persistent, criticised and attacked for several centuries before it was finally demoted. Leonardo da Vinci had refused, in the fifteenth century, to 'lie

5

as though dead upon the spoils of other dead creatures: by sleeping upon the feathers of birds.' Thomas Tryon, in *The Way to Health, Long Life, and Happiness*, 1683, was sickened by the '*Unclean, fulsom Excrement*' of feathers which, though attractive to bugs, forced the sleeper 'to keep his Nose above-board.' Leigh Hunt was still sunk in the 'Slough of Despond' in 1847, waiting for his 'repose and independence' to be rescued from the 'hands of /this/ soft luberly giant.'

Demands for healthy hardness have not ceased–not even for the small comforts recommended by so expert a bed-goer as Dr. Marie Stopes, our pioneer of planned parenthood. Whether she settled on horsehair (in use since the seventeenth century), interior boxed-springs, or an air mattress, like the *lit de vent* made for Louis XI in 1478, we do not know. Nothing, however, would have induced her to have a foam-rubber mattress or rubber tyred wheels on the bed, for they insulate the earth's electric currents with which, she believed, continuous contact is essential. Unfortunately, the water bed did not appear in time to prove its excellence as a conductor.

Blankets too have been subject to the whims of fashion. The Greeks prized those from Corinth; Romans preferred Leuconian wool, imported from the Meuse valley, with a passion for Assyrian purple which, according to Pliny, was so much used on beds that it became unfashionable for togas. The best medieval blankets, or fustians, were from Chalons in France. Since antiquity, quilts have been used both as mattresses and as warm and decorative covers, flourished with threads of gold or thriftily patchworked. The only innovation in blankets, a questionable one at that, is the electric one. The duvets that currently threaten to displace all covers and counterpanes are no different from the feather-beds which our Northern European ancestors slept on and under.

Sheets fitted tightly across the mattress are not only a blessing to busy bed-makers, but have recently become a lively field for high fashion designers. Now that we can all afford to lie on an exotic ground adapted for Marks and Spencer from a seventeenth-century Persian prayer mat in the Victoria and Albert Museum, we may be less impressed by the fine linen of the Pharaohs; sweet-scented Roman sheets; sixteenth-century sheets hemmed with gold thread for Henry III of France: the two thousand crowns worth of linen, trimmed with *point de Venise* and embroidered with *chiffres*, presented to the bride of Leopold Joseph, Duc de Lorraine in 1698; or even the black satin chosen by some Renaissance ladies better to display the whiteness of their skin.

Pillows, like mattresses, have been the subject of centuries of debate which the stoics, concerned with spinal straightness, have won. Although their shape and contents have altered little since antiquity, their number has certainly dwindled. The Greeks had plenty of richly embroidered cushions and bolsters on which to rest their head and feet; Persians and other Near Easterners had even more and richer ones. The two or three recommended by Dr. Stopes was long-standing tradition, but the eighteen supposedly used by Enrico Caruso, all at once, is excessive. One is now considered the healthy rule.

Before complaining, think of the rigid head (or neck) rests that served as pillows in Egypt, China, Northwest India, Africa and Polynesia. Ideas of comfort obviously rest in the head; indeed, it was for the welfare of the head that these rests were intended. The Egyptians, regarding the head as the seat of life, were prepared to lavish no end of attention on a prop which not only would keep it cool and well preserved, but, if elaborated with appropriate gods, and spells from the *Book of the Dead*, would ensure its continued existence in after-life. Between Chinese heads and pillows there was a more direct and animated communication. Softness, it was thought, robbed vitality. Hard and cool wood, leather and ceramic pillows brought gloss to the living as well as the dead. Filled with specified herbal concoctions, appropriately decorated or inscribed (the Ai-shan pillow, *[fig.1]*, promises good results), they could counteract ill-winds, cure disease, cause white hair to turn black, restore lost teeth, and inspire sweet dreams.

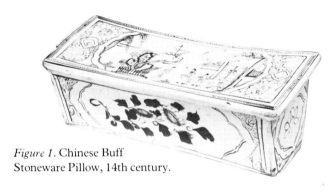

Figure 1. Chinese Buff
Stoneware Pillow, 14th century.

A Bedstead (or bedstock)–a special place for a bed–is, as the
Japanese well know, an unnecessary luxury. It contributes little
to the function of a bed, physical rest and well-being, though it
may rest the mind to be above the creatures that crawl on the
ground. Since the Middle Ages, it has had but one role, a minor
one in support of the mattress, covers and curtains, which were
the more important and costly elements. Its materials and
ornaments have varied–so too have methods of joinery–but its
fundamental structure is stereotyped: a long rectangular frame
interlaced with cords, thongs or webbing, or filled-in with hide,
canvas or boards, and raised on four or more legs. Spiral springs,
long used in carriages, were eventually adapted to beds in the
nineteenth century, first in flat wire-mesh mattresses, and
subsequently in coils boxed in upholstered bases. These inno-
vations greatly improved the durability, resilience and hygiene
of the bed.

Ancient bedsteads, unlike their modern successors, were
independent objects of considerable significance, endowed with
magical properties, or used day and night for multiple purposes.
The beds of the Pharaohs, like many other earthly Egyptian
possessions, appear to have been expressly prepared to deliver
their occupants into the long awaited after-life. Gently raised at
the head, or concave in the centre, they were carried on animal
legs, some sheathed in gold, others richly carved, painted or
inlaid. Normally, a foot board was provided, perhaps to prevent

8

the tilted sleeper from slipping off. Never was there anything to constrain the head where life was believed to be seated.

The Greek *kline*, *[fig. 2]* or couch, used both for sleeping and for reclining at meals, was a major article of household furniture. It was not, however, an ordinary one, for reclining was a privilege of gentlemen and their courtesans, which women and slaves did not share. Couch-making was a distinguished trade, and the products of some centres, Miletus and Chios for example, were more highly prized than others. Unlike an Egyptian bed, the *kline* had a low head rest to prop the mattress and pillows, but no foot board. Its wooden frame, on turned, rectangular or animal legs, was decorated with ornaments of ivory, tortoise shell, gold, silver or bronze. Alexander the Great is said to have slept on a golden couch in a tent supported by fifty golden columns. His Persian predecessors were accustomed to lie in far greater splendour on golden beds beneath gilded vines laden with grapes of precious stones.

The Etruscans kept the *kline* more or less as it was, but allowed their women equal rights of use. The Romans increased and perfected luxurious lounging with separate couches for specific purposes: a *lectus cubicularis* for sleeping; a *lectus grabatus* for indigent sleepers; a *lectus triclinium* for dining, and other *lecti* for reading and writing. Although distinguished by name and function, these couches did not differ much in form. Turned legs, ornamental inlays, and bronze mounts (usually

Figure 2. The Greek *Kline* used for dining and sleeping. Detail from a Greek red figured kylix by the painter, Douris.
Volci, c.500–470 B.C.

Figure 3. High-backed Roman couch on which a dead girl lies surrounded by mourners. Roman Sarcophagus, 2nd century A.D.

equine) were common to all. There were two types for sleep: one with a head and foot board, the other, a new innovation, was raised on three sides and occasionally upholstered like a sofa *[fig.3]*. A married couple spent their wedding night in a larger *lectus genialis* which was afterwards moved to the other side of the atrium and called a *lectus adversus*. Most antique couches were lightweight and portable. Such was the bed on which the paralytic was lowered though the roof tiles to Christ to be cured, and which he was then ordered to pick up and carry home *[fig.4]*.

The Chinese had their own equivalent to the *kline*, the *k'ang*, a built-in or moveable platform used as a bed, table and seat, under-heated, in the north, by flues from a central furnace. Later variations include a free-standing, compartmented edifice that functioned as a complete living unit within a room *[pl.1]*.

Figure 4. The Paralytic healed by Christ carries his bed home. Detail, The Miracles of Christ. Ivory, Italian (Rome), 450–60 A.D.

2 Fashions in Beds

Your bed is in many ways a representation of you. It has a body–a mattress; undergarments–sheets and blankets; and 'next to the human cheek', in Leigh Hunt's pun, pillows. These are essential, private parts where life comes and goes. They are not for public viewing. Robert Rauschenberg's *Bed*, his own quilt and pillow defiled by paint and exhibited as a work of Pop Art in 1955, had a deeply disturbing effect upon its viewers. The bed is a highly sensitive subject. To be secure within, decent and presentable without, it must don a full suit of clothing –curtains, coverlet and canopy. Whatever may be seen of the seat, or bedstead, on which the bed is privileged to sit, it is never more important than the fully dressed sitter. No, the clothes make the bed as they do the man. The style of dress, the volume, richness, cut and trim of the fabric announce the bed's rank and quality; enable it to be distinguished from others of different date and origin; suggest a name–French bed, canopy bed, *lit clos*, *lit à la romaine* or some other. The clothes will provide a history of the whole species.

Ancient Beds, though scantily dressed by later standards, were never without a fine curtain to keep out gnats and mosquitos. Queen Herepheres, mother of Cheops, hung hers on a gilded frame to form a canopied chamber. Poorer Egyptians, Herodotus said, would crawl into bed under a fishing net. Vulcan can be seen laying a net over his marital couch to catch his unfaithful wife, Venus, frolicking with Ares *[fig.5]*. Natives of India were observed by Marco Polo pulling strings to draw the airy curtains which protected their beds from the miniscule mosquitos, magnified by translators since the sixteenth century into 'tarantulas, . . . fleas and other small vermin.' The classical Latin *canopeum*, 'a net of fine gauze about the bed, a mosquito curtain', is the source of our word canopy.

From the Middle Ages to the Eighteenth Century, after the fall of the Roman Empire, Western European beds retired in a cocoon of hangings from which none but a few emerged. In the insecure, unstable and underpopulated world recovering from barbarian invasions, protection and mobility were, for those who could afford them, the first and foremost requirements of life. Only the rich had household furniture, and then very little of it. They certainly had nothing that was at once as protective of their physical well-being and as portable as bed furnishings. The bedstead, unless it was a collapsible, trussing bed of which many are recorded, was a crude, worthless structure that was often left behind and eventually destroyed or dismantled for other uses. Bed hangings, on the contrary, were second only to the fabric of the house as objects of great expenditure and elaboration; as insignia of material sucess, and as heirlooms of everlasting value *[pl.2, 3 and fig.6]*.

Look at the fragments of medieval and Renaissance hangings

Figure 5. Vulcan laying a net on his nuptial bed to catch his unfaithful wife, Venus. Tapestry, English (Mortlake) 17th century, copied from a Brussels tapestry of the 16th century.

Figure 6. Media and Jason in a round canopied bed with a cassone before it. Detail, Stove Tile, South Tyrolese (probably Bolzano), c.1546.

n the Victoria and Albert Museum, remembering that yards and yards were required to cover but one bed. Read the colourful descriptions of curtains and counterpanes in contemporary inventories. The splendour of beds 'covered with ermine', beds of white 'silk, with blue eagles displayed', beds of 'red velvet, embroidered with ostrich feathers of silver, and heads of leopards of gold' is overwhelming. It is little wonder that the Earl of Arundel thought it fitting to distinguish his precious bed by name, Clove; that travellers in the seventeenth century continued to carry their favourite beds with them; that the best bed was the great prize of a forfeited estate, and a new marriage bed the perquisite of the head of the bedchamber. An expensive bed, however acquired, might well be the future salvation, or at least a momento, of a family's fortune. Thomas Hungerford, Knight, did well to stipulate that the 'next heire' of his two beds of cloth of gold and one of tapestry work called 'the bed of bestis with cattis of the mountayne' should 'leve the said beddes with all their appurtenances to his next heire . . . that for all wayes as long as the said beddes will endure they remayne from heire to heire in worship and memory of my lord, my father, Walter, Lord Hungerford, that first ordeyned them and paid for them.'

The price of a bed that needed remembering in the fifteenth century could not be forgotten by the eighteenth century. The £1200 lavished by Robert Walpole just on the gold lace for his Green Velvet bed at Houghton was almost double the sum spent in 1714 on the cut velvet for Queen Anne's bed at Windsor Castle. There can be no better statement of the values of the past than the comparative estimates in 1651 of Charles I's bed of richly embroidered green satin, worth £1000, and his Raphael cartoons, worth only £300.

Such splendour, though desired by all, was limited to those at the top. Most beds, like most sleepers, were perfectly respectable and equally well protected in simpler apparel. Gold lace was hardly essential, and there were many alternatives to rich Genoese velvets and Lyons silks. The best native fabrics cost much less than equivalent imported ones. Linen could be

painted or printed to resemble tapestry or silk damask; there
were counterfeit brocades, and a wide range of woollens some
as fine as cheaper silks. Wood panelling, or just three bare walls
with a curtain or two made a very inexpensive and cosy
cupboard or bunk bed for sleepers in Scotland, Brittany,
Scandinavia, the greek islands, and elsewhere *[fig.7]*. The
truckle (trundle or wheel) bed, a fifteenth-century innovation
which pulled out from under a great bed for the use of servants,
might not be draped at all. A collapsible wood or metal frame
with a loose cover made a camp bed, a *lit de campagne*, fit,
according to the quality and enrichment of the cover, for a king
or commoner *[fig.8]*.

Any respectably dressed bed would have above it a round
canopy, or more often a rectangular one, called a tester, covering
its whole or half length, either suspended from the ceiling
(sparver), or supported on posts. Every visible part of this
superstructure would be masked by fabrics. The posts had

Figure 7. A Man in a Cupboard Bed, his warming pan hanging at the
end, his chamber pot on the chair beside him. Johannes de Brunes,
Emblemata of Zinne-werck, Amsterdam, 1624, p.101.

14

Figure 8. A Camp Bed. Thomas Sheraton, *Cabinet Maker's Dictionary*, 1803, pl.15.

cases, and the whole of the tester was upholstered–the underside or ceiling, the top if it rose to a dome, and the edges inside and out with valances. Standing on top were corner finials, simple 'bobbs' or elaborate cups filled with panaches of ostrich plumes. At the head hung a head cloth (dossier) with or without a head board behind it; and around the three sides at least three, at most six, and usually four curtains, a narrow pair enclosing the head and a wider pair for the sides and foot. The corners, where three or six curtains met, were protected from draughts by quarter strips, 'cantoons', or 'bonegraces' flanking the head. The bedstead was concealed by base valances; the mattress, bedding and bolster by a neatly fitting counterpane trimmed to allow for the posts, and, in particular cases, rigidly corseted with rods or stays. A careful arrangement of large and small cushions covered in matching fabric provided the final flourish.

While the accoutrements of the bed had enormous scope for variety, the overall shape had little. Like the shell of a house, it was comparatively limited in design. By the seventeenth century the simple rectangular profile of the so-called 'French bedde' had become standard for beds of all classes throughout Europe *[fig.9]*. Owing, however, to the deterioration of textile hangings and the destruction of insignificant wooden frames, few examples of this type have survived intact. We are very much

15

Figure 9. l'Accouchée, Abraham Bosse (1602–1676), Engraving. French.

Figure 10. The Great Bed of Ware, c.1590, probably made for the White Hart Inn, Ware, Herts. First mentioned by name in Shakespeare's Twelfth Night, 1601.

more familiar with the carved four-posters of the sixteenth century and, therefore, are inclined to attach more importance to them than they had in their own time. These edifices, conceived by Italian Renaissance architects, were elaborated and publicized by Jacques Androuet du Cerceau in France and Hans Vredeman de Vries in Holland, and culminated in the Great Bed of Ware *[fig.10]*. After a relatively short and unsuccessful life, the vogue vanished, only to be resurrected by Tudor revivalists of the nineteenth century. Wood, however richly carved and inlaid, could never compete with sumptuous textiles.

Full dress remained *de rigueur* for beds. But by the end of the seventeenth century the rigid silhouette imposed by French fashion had become too restrictive to Dutch and English court tastes. The urge for expansion was promptly satisfied by the taller, more voluptuous baroque beds designed by Daniel Marot, architect to William of Orange (later William III) *[fig.11]*. The fifteen foot tall Marotesque bed, made in 1692 for the Earl of Melville, one of William's courtiers, with elaborately scrolled and branching parts all draped, fringed and festooned

Figure 11. State Bed and Bedchamber, Daniel Margot. Engraving, Dutch, 1702. The bed is provided with a rod for case covers.

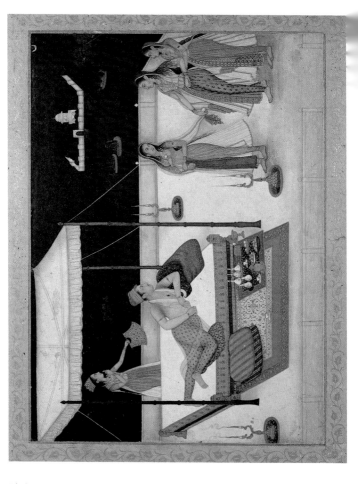

Plate 1. Prince Murad Baksh receiving a lady at night. Mughal miniature, 1680–90.

18

Plate 2. The Birth of the Virgin, showing St Anne in a half tester bed with the Virgin's wooden rocker beside it. Detail. Playfair Book of Hours, N. French, c.1475.

19

Plate 3 (left). The Birth of Essau. Limoges plate, painted with coloured grisaille and translucent enamels on copper. French. Jean de Court, c.1560. Detail. The bed is in the style of Du Cerceau. Salting Bequest.

Plate 4. Chinoiserie Bed from Badminton House, Glos., made c.1750 for Elizabeth Berkeley, Duchess of Beaufort. English, attributed to John Linnell.

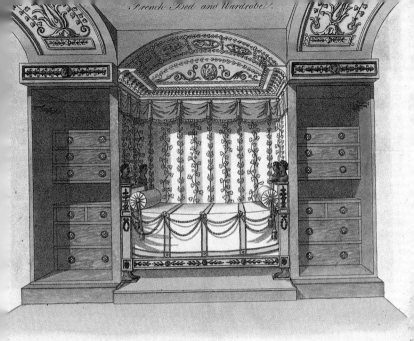

London. Published Dec.1.1804.by J.Taylor, N°.59 High Holborn.

Plate 5 (left). State Bed, Osterley Park, designed by Robert Adam for Robert Child, 1776. The bed hangings, bed carpet and chairs are en suite with the decoration of the room. The counterpane shown here is not original.

Plate 6. French Bed and Wardrobe. Designed by George Smith, 1804. An early example of built-in furniture, more practical than Percier and Fortaine's design by which it is inspired. Engraving from G. Smith, *Designs for Household Furniture*, London, 1808. pl. 32.

in a dramatic contrast of white silk damask and crimson velvet, is a grandiose stage set devised not for mundane use but for ceremonial viewing *[fig.12]*.

State Beds: To make a bed fit for a king is no problem. A peaceful and private place to put it was more difficult to find as European courts continued to expand from the Middle Ages to the seventeenth century. The answer–condensing into a few words a long and complicated social and architectural evolution–was the creation under one roof of two complete households: a private Apartment (one for the king, another for the queen) and a State Apartment. The latter, though intended for court use, always included, among other rooms, a State Bedchamber. The rôle and position of this room were as different in England and France as the concept of monarchy itself.

In France the power of the king was expressed by his public presence. Louis XIV's absolute power was asserted by his omnipresence, by a fusion of his private, social and state rôles. He was the only French king to sleep in state. The State Bedchamber, normally only a symbolic sleeping place, was always the focal point of court life, the principal reception room for Levées, the place where ambassadors and other visitors were received. This court custom was imitated, indeed rivalled in the châteaux of the nobility. It became common practice for ladies to receive social visits, condolences and congratulations reclining in bed. The Duc de Chaumal had a fountain in his State Bedchamber not to induce sleep but to entertain his guests.

The royal bed was even more widely emulated than the bedroom. But its position within the room and the respect it commanded were sacred to the king. His bed was the equivalent of his throne. In parliament his seat of honour was a canopied arrangement of cushions called a *lit de Justice*. In the State Bedchamber his bed stood on a raised dais, a *parquet*, under a special canopy. Like an altar, it was set apart from the rest of the room, *en tribunal*, by a balustrade which could not be touched by anyone, and could only be imitated by members of the royal family. The enclosed space, whether or not it contained a bed,

Figure 12. State Bed from Melville House, Fife. Designed in 1692 for George, 1st Earl of Melville (1636–1707).

was kept sacrosanct under the strict surveillance of a *Valet de Chambre*. Anyone entering the room, royalty included, was required to salute the bed or its enclosure.

The State Apartment of the constitutional monarch of England was the scene of much greater, more regulated ceremonial, devised not to present but to separate king and courtiers. A long and strictly prescribed enfilade of State, public reception, and private rooms filtered visitors according to their rank. The State Bedchamber was almost the most private of private rooms, penultimate to the inner sanctum of government, the king's Closet, with access limited to those permitted to enter the Closet. Only for a brief period under Charles II was the State Bedchamber used, as it was in France, for reception. At no time was the royal State Bed slept in. It might be raised on a dais but did not have to be. Gentlemen of the Bedchamber stationed at the foot of the bed and at the entrance to the room were normally considered sufficient protection. The balustrade observed by Celia Fiennes before the state bed at Nottingham Castle was unusual.

The spatial arrangement of the royal State Apartment was imitated in great country houses like Chatsworth, Burghley and Boughton. Here, where there was no royal ceremonial, the state bedchamber and bed became the dramatic climax of a processional route. It was slept in only by the most honoured visitors, and, except for christenings, was never used for reception. It was, like an armorial bearing, a visible symbol of the rank and social distinction of its owner. By the middle of the eighteenth century parades of grandeur were outmoded. Pretentiousness was the prime motive for Walpole's expensive state bed at Houghton and Robert Child's at Osterley [pl.5].

Eighteenth and early Nineteenth-century Beds: Ever since 'God said let there be Newton, and all was light' things have looked very different. Further scientific investigations, improvements in technology, commerce and communication shed more and more light on the world, bringing men closer to it and to each other. Life became altogether more relaxed, more intimate and informal. Mammoth piles like Versailles and Blenheim gave way to smaller villas, town houses, or *hôtels*; interminable straight avenues were abandoned for confounding serpentines and natural landscapes. And so too, beds came down from Marotesque heights to a more human scale. Instead of dominating their surroundings, they were integrated into them, or secreted in alcoves.

Fashion stole the show from fortune. An insatiable appetite for variety and novelty was fed by a succession of styles: Chinese, gothic, classical, Egyptian, Pompeian, rustic and baronial, military and naval, accurately archaeological and fancifully romantic [pls.4 and 5]. Just as Robert Adam's experience of Roman ruins provided the bed at Osterley with a 'modern head-dress' that Horace Walpole thought would have horrified Vitruvius, so Napaleon's campaigns in Egypt brought enough sphinxes and swords to beds to terrify the Pharaohs.

Fashion ruled without social barriers, universally disseminated by engravings, pattern books, trade catalogues, and later by industrial exhibitions.

A wider variety of structural materials (mahogany imported from the colonies; native woods, veneered, lacquered, japanned, gilded and painted); and new machine-powered tools for sawing boards, slicing veneers, and cutting screws brought more freedom to designers and makers of beds. Production increased; cost and quality decreased. The hitherto hidden bedstead gained greater importance. Posts were made to be seen, and the four-poster remained the most common, but not always the most fashionable type of bed. Head and foot boards assumed stylish prominence; alcove beds, long side to the wall, generally had a raised back as well, like ancient Roman couches.

While extensions and elaborations of the frame went in and out of fashion, canopy and curtains remained, at least until the second half of the nineteenth century, a constant theme upon which numerous variations were played. There were domical canopies (round and square) either raised on curved iron rods concealed by the curtains (*lit à la polonaise [fig.13], à la dauphine, à la romaine, à l'Italienne*, etc.), or fixed to the wall for a *lit à l'anglaise* or *à la turque*. Testers–large, *à la duchesse* or small, *d' ange* projected out from the head; sloped to the foot in military fashion, *lit de campagne*, or with abrupt finality *en tombeau*. There were many other ingenious alternatives, artfully draped poles and wall brackets among them. Hangings, however arranged, were required not only to provide privacy and protection, but above all to create a *mise-en-scène* around the bed *[pl.6 and fig.14]*. The imposing opulence of the past was cast off for coquettish confections. Though there were moments of military and archaeological masculinity, they too bowed to the dominant female fashions.

'Velvet, and such like cumbrous clouds, lording it over the sweet idea of rest' disgusted Leigh Hunt and his contemporaries. The general preference was for smoother, lighter textiles: silks and satins for the very rich and, down the scale, taffetas, chintz, calico, linsey and so on. Those who delighted in chinoiserie

Figure 13 (left). Lit à la polonaise. French (Paris), c.1780. Stamped G. Jacob. The pale blue silk damask hangings with silver fringe are original.

Figure 14. A Pompeian style bedroom with the bed raised like an altar in a Temple of Diana. Executed in Paris to designs by C. Percier and P.-F.-L. Fontaine. Engraving from Percier and Fontaine, *Recueil de Décorations Intérieures*, Paris, 1812 (1st edition 1801), pl.25.

maintained the seventeenth-century taste for Indian fabrics painted and later printed with exotic eastern designs. Most, however, wanted delicate 'flowery curtains' or plain, unobtrusive colours. It was the custom for ladies, since the days of Athene, to lavish their talents with the needle or loom on the beauty of the bed. Domestic needlework, though it lost some of its past perfection, continued to flourish well into the eighteenth century. All the beds of state at Badminton were embroidered, trimmed, and finished in the house. Queen Charlotte made fringes; Mrs. Delany knotted tassels; Lady Mary Vyvyan embroidered an exquisite counterpane and cushions while imprisoned in the Tower of London in 1715 *[fig.15]*. Girls in the Greek Islands of Cos and Rhodes embroidered intricate patterns over curtains and covers for their marriage beds *[pl.7]*. Puritan American ladies put all their thrift and industry into transforming scraps of material into bold patchworks to keep themselves warm, and to equip their daughters with the thirteen quilts that completed a wedding 'hope' chest *[pl.8]*. At the other extreme, new and better machines for spinning and weaving; improvements in the chemistry and mechanics of dyeing produced masses of decorative fabrics to suit every taste and purse. And as the supply of fabrics increased, so drapes and festoons, simplified in the beginnings of the eighteenth and nineteenth centuries, proliferated and became nightmarishly complex.

Figure 15. Coverlet, Part of a set of bed furnishings, including pillows and cushions, embroidered by Mary, wife of Sir Richard Vyvyan of Trelowarren, when she and her husband were imprisoned in the Tower of London in 1715.

Leigh Hunt might not have complained in 1847 of 'the cut-and-dry look . . . the cheap sufficiency . . . the cold precision' of the Grecian style had he foreseen the suffocating fashion that was to follow it [fig.16].

The Bed in the last Hundred Years has radically changed its appearance. Whether it has progressed or regressed is a philosophical question that might be better turned over leisurely in bed than hurriedly here.

Beds 'forged of iron, gilded' were known in ancient Pompeii, and were described by John Evelyn in 1645 as the most common Italian solution to the problem of bed bugs. Some two hundred years later the brass beds that invaded millions of English homes were looked upon as shining signals of progress. It took an Industrial Revolution to provide the masses with both tubular

Figure 16. A bedroom suffocated by upholstery. The bed with a loose fitting counterpane in the style 'negligée', behind intricate corner curtains. The walls, windows, mantle-piece, and furniture all fully draped; the floor covered with patterned close carpeting. Engraving from Jules Verdellet, *Manuel Gèometrique du Tapissier*, Paris, end ed. 1864 (1st ed. 1859), pl. 29.

Figure 17 (left). Healthy Brass Beds. Engraving from Lady Barker, *The Bedroom and Boudoir*, London, 1878, p. 37.

Figure 18. A Brass Four-Poster in the 'Renaissance' style, By R. W. Winfield of Birmingham. Exhibited in the Great Exhibition, 1851. From M. D. Wyatt, *Industrial Arts of the 19th Century*, London, 1851, pl. 43.

metal bedsteads and living conditions unhealthy enough to make them a necessity. Most of the first metal bedsteads, patented and produced in the 1830s, went into hospitals, prisons, workhouses, schools, and the few dwellings designed especially for the labouring classes. Interest in standards of health and hygiene, initially focused on situations, like the Crimea, where they did not exist at all, soon spread to all ranks and aspects of civil life from the corset to the bed. Four-posters, the 'majestic microb-traps' of old, were tumbled by humanitarians and sanitarians who replaced them with thousands of clean and cheerful brass beds off the Birmingham production lines *[fig.17]*. London's lady inhabitants were instructed by R. W. Edis to let in light and fresh air, remove their dusty bed curtains, and create a 'general home feeling of rest and comfort, by innumerable knick-knacks.' Most of them did as told. Those addicted to fashion applied their feminine ingenuity to fitting the simple brass frame with swinging screens covered with glossy, dust repellent satin, or draping the walls instead. Great industrial potentates were able to display their riches with cast metal edifices every bit as imposing as the old-fashioned wooden ones *[fig.18]*.

The machine made brass beds that wealthy manufacturers and healthy customers looked upon as exemplars of enlightened progress were despised by artists–followers of William Morris in England and Comte Léon de Laborde in France–as the extinction of Ruskin's 'lamp of truth', the degradation and destruction of the very essence of civilization–human art and labour. Simultaneously the Arts and Crafts Movement and Art Nouveau orchestrated a revival of natural materials, quality craftsmanship and artistic decoration, based on medieval traditions like Norman Shaw's cradle and William Burges's carved

Figure 19. Art Nouveau Bedroom Suite by la Maison Mercier Frères, exhibited in the *Salon du Mobilier de 1902*, Paris, 1903, pl.12.

and painted bed inlaid with illuminated vellum and glass [pl.9]; or breaking new ground with ornaments composed of sinuous stems and other plant forms, like the bedroom suite exhibited in Paris in 1902 by la Maison Mercier [fig.19]. By the end of the nineteenth century the artistic creations conceived to counter commercialism were being commercially produced and marketed by progressive firms like Heal's and Liberty's.

Today, only the historically initiated remember Burges and Shaw. Sir Ambrose Heal is honoured as the harbinger of honest wooden bedsteads [fig.20]; defended by Nikolaus Pevsner against the succeeding generation, the 'misguided supporters of modernistic forms.' But modernism has contributed little or nothing to the form of the bed. It has finished what the health fanatics started: the negation of the bedstead and the return to the first essential, the mattress. A head board is the only modern concession to design, and even that is no longer an integral part of the bed. It is a built-in wall fixture complete with lights, music and every conceivable convenience. What use are curtains if the turn of a switch will heat the room and the bed.

The vast quantity of time consumed by a bed is now of less

Figure 20. Heal's Bedroom Suite, late 1870s.

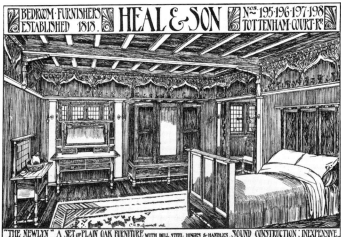

interest than its greedy consumption of valuable space. The preoccupation of twentieth-century designers with space saving combination furniture, useable night and day, has a long pedigree dating back to the ancient Greek *kline*. In 1644 Evelyn saw two 'conceited chayres' in Rome, one of them in the Palazzo de Medici which turned 'into a bed, a bolster, a Table, a Couch.' Simple eighteenth-century 'press' beds that tipped up into a cupboard were the forerunners of show pieces like the American 'parlour' beds *[fig.21]*. There were many nineteenth-century sofa beds *[fig.22]* before Alvar Aalto's tubular steel refinement *[fig.23]*. Of all the bizarre combinations, bed fireplaces, bed bookcases and tables, the 'mimicries' distinguished by Geidion from the 'metamorphoses' of bed-sofa, there is none to equal the 1866 piano bed. A mattress in a drawer where the pedals are, a bureau, storage chests, wash bowl, pitcher and so forth 'did not in the least impair its qualities as a musical instrument.'

Figure 21. American 'Parlour Bed in richly figured Mahogany with full-length beveled mirror in front, Colonial desk dressing-table in mahogany to match', and a table-night-table-wash-stand. From *The Decorator and Furnisher*, New York, April 1891, XVIII, p. 19.

Figure 22(above).
Convertible 'Sofa Bed' by
Thomas Sheraton
published in *The Cabinet
Dictionary*, London, 1803,
pl. 17.

Figure 23. Alvar Aalto,
tubular steel convertible
sofa bed, 1932.

3 Beds for Marriage, Birth and Death

The stage for marriage, birth, death and mourning was a bed suitably attired for a performance before an invited audience.

The Marriage Bed, now no different from the one the night before or any other, in the past was always specially decorated for the occasion. At the Jewish wedding which Evelyn attended in Venice in 1646, the bed 'was dress'd up with flowers, and the counterpane strew'd in workes.' The Phoenicians inlaid the panels of their nuptial couches with erotic subjects courting fertility. European nobles spent fortunes on ostentatious hangings; American brides brought out the thirteenth patchwork quilt while those in Rhodes hung their newest and best embroidered curtains across the bunk. The bedchamber, often decorated as well, was now ready to receive guests gathered either to witness the formal union of royal minors, in person or by proxy, or festively to escort the newly-weds to bed. That done, the party normally ended. Not, however, in France where, on the following day, the bride was expected to be in bed for another visitation. In England, the once used nuptial bed became the formal perquisite of the Master of the Bedchamber, the informal object of barter.

Birth comes next: the most important of all events: the beginning of new life; the consummation of marriage, the extension of a consolidated family, the vital moment of a dynasty. It is an occasion that is always celebrated and frequently depicted, sometimes in anticipation of future distinction, more often, for gods and heroes, after it had been achieved. The scene of the celebration was again the bed, well dressed for show but not necessarily with the extravagance of the Countess of Salisbury's, draped with fourteen thousands pounds worth of white satin embroidered with silver and pearls in honour of the birth of a daughter in 1612. Let us not, however, forget the object of this celebration, the infant whose small bed was every bit as important as his mother's large one.

Cradles, unlike bedsteads, were portable and therefore more susceptible to the kinds of elaboration (carving, inlay, painting, gilding, etc.) afforded to other articles of furniture, chests in particular which they closely resemble both in shape and construction *[fig.24]*. As a rule, they were also made of better materials, with certain woods being favoured for legendary advantages: birch, the tree of inception, repellent to evil spirits more than elder which attracts them; and later, in the nineteenth century, wicker for its hygienic properties. A soothing sway, the universal requirement of infants whether bedded or not, was provided either by mounting the cradle on low rockers, an improvement upon the primitive hollowed log, or by suspending it from fixed vertical posts. The latter is occasionally called a cot. So too is the canvas hammock used at sea, a subject which will not be considered here. Rocking the baby is a labour of love which was never to be replaced by labour-saving gadgets like the mechanical rocker published by Sheraton in 1803. The motionless crib is aptly defined by the *Oxford English Dictionary* as a barred receptacle both for children and fodder. Many of the

Figure 24. Cradle designed c.1867 for Julian Waterhouse, born 1868, one of the sons of the architect, Alfred Waterhouse.

nineteenth-century metal barred cribs were veritable cages, guaranteed to be escape proof.

The hierarchy that we have seen in adult bedding begins in infancy where, it seems, the weaker the flesh, the stronger and more ornate was the cradle. The holiest of infants had the simplest of all, a bed of straw in a manger, or at best a Moses basket of plaited rushes. Children of mortal descent, even the young Virgin, needed something a bit more solid, a simple wooden basin or rocker. For royal progeny, male heirs in particular, no luxury was too great, nor was one cradle sufficient. Two were required, one for ordinary use but not of ordinary appearance, and another still richer and larger for ceremonial reception, a '*berceau de parade*' or 'cradell of estate'. The regulation 'litell cradell' of a fifteenth-century prince or princess was one foot (30.5cm) wide and three feet eight inches (1.12m) long, a narrow trough, carved, gilded, capped with finials of silver and gold, and fitted with silver buckles to strap the swaddled infant in. The state cradle was to be almost twice as large (the size of an adult's single bed) and elaborate. George IV, in his infancy, went on public display in a golden cradle covered with crimson velvet and gold lace. The King of Rome had a cradle of silver and lapis, designed by Prud'hon and presented to him by the City of Paris *[pl.10]*. But he lay in the Tuilleries in a simplified version with ormolu mounts, costing his father, Napoleon, six thousand francs.

Regardless of rank, all cradles, like beds, were protected, at least during the day, by curtains draped from the hood as from a tester, or hung from a suspended canopy or standing post. At night the cradle might share the curtains and the vapours of the nurse's or mother's bed. The quality of the coverings displayed, as usual, the rank and riches of the parents. Margaret of Flanders' children lay in the fifteenth century under a coral counterpane trimmed with 1200 ermine skins. Queen Mary's cradle had a gaudy counterpane of yellow cloth of gold and crimson velvet lined with green, a valance fringed with blue and red silk mixed with Venice gold, and four blue and red curtains. Most children in the past, and some in the present too, were more gorgeously and unhealthfully encased than adults, in curtains, covers, caps, swaddles, and clothes, in airless, over-heated rooms about which they were unable to complain. Fortunately, their parents have awakened to their plight, some, like Evelyn, too late, for his five-year-old son died in 1658 because 'the woman maide that tended him, and covered him too hott with blankets as he lay in a cradle, neere an excessive hot fire in a close roome.'

The Death Bed is not a very attractive subject, nor one that need detail us *[pl.11]*. It is the mourning bed that invites onlookers, the catafalque too, though it is technically not a bed. The bereaved, dressed in black, traditionally received condolences and slept, during the period of mourning, in a black bed, in a room lugubriously draped from floor to ceiling in black cloth, and furnished down to the smallest detail–fire tongs and shovel–in black. Liselotte, Duchess of Orleans, sister-in law of Louis XIV, provides a detailed and somewhat irreverent description of the 'ghastly sight' of the ceremonial condolence paid her by the exiled King and Queen of England at Versailles in 1701. Dressed and hooded in 'the strangest apparel' of black cloth and yards of ermine trimmings, she was arranged 'to show the ermine' on a 'black bed in an entirely blackened room. Even the *parquet* was covered in black and the windows hung with crêpe.' All her domestics stood by wearing 'long mourning coats; forty or fifty ladies, all in crêpe.' This vast quantity of gloomy paraphernalia had to be multiplied many times to cover the whole of a household. Death in a large house was an extremely expensive business. Some families, like the Verneys of Claydon, kept a store of mourning equipment which they lent to friends and relations. Many, of all ranks, hired the decorations, at least for their London houses, from funeral providers. The velvet bed of state, 380 yards of black velvet, and many other furnishings for Marlborough House were hired in 1722 for the thirty-five days of mourning for the famous Duke. The black bedroom furniture hired for Southampton House on the death of the second Duke of Bedford remained there for two years; the other furnishings for only one.

Deceased persons of rank or distinction were not only mourned in bed, their corpses or effigies were also displayed on ceremonial funeral beds, in accordance with ancient custom. For the lying-in-state of Queen Mary II in 1695, described by Celia Fiennes as one of the 'most renowned that ever was', an elaborate canopied bed of purple velvet, richly fringed, painted, and embroidered with gold, was erected in Whitehall on a draped dais, 'railed as the manner of the princes beds are', and watched over by a changing guard of '4 Ladyes of the Bed Chamber – Countesses – with vailes' *[fig.25]*.

Figure 25. Queen Mary II Lying-In-State in February 1695. Engraved from a drawing by Romeyn de Hooge commissioned by William III. Published by Sammuel Grutero, *Funeralia Mariae II,* Amsterdam, 1695, pl. 16 detail.

4 Caring for The Bed

No article of household furniture demands as much attention as the bed. Its clothes must be frequently laundered and cleaned; every morning in Japan they must be folded and stored away; aired and rearranged in most other parts of the world. This humdrum task of housekeeping originated in the fifth century B.C. as an honoured profession. The bed-loving Persians were, according to Heraclides, the first to have particular servants to make their beds. One of these servants was included in the gift of a silver-footed bed with expensive coverlets, which Timagoras the Cretan received from King Artaxerxes who believed that the 'Greeks did not know how to arrange a couch.' Roman lovers of luxury were quick to learn the Persian lesson. The services of 'Titus Flavius, freedman of Augustus Caesar, in charge of the bed clothes' were worth remembering on a tombstone. But caring for Caesar's beds seems like child's play compared to the heavy duty required by the ponderous cocoons introduced in the Middle Ages.

The royal Bedchamber had its own regimental hierarchy of attendants from a Master Chamberlain to Ushers, Grooms, Yeomen Valets (of which Chaucer was one), and Squires who together made the bed according to ordained procedure. Thus, a bed fit for Henry VII required a Gentleman Usher to draw the curtains; a Groom to carry in fresh straw; a Squire and Yeoman to truss, lay and test it for concealed weapons, cover it with canvas, a feather bed, sheets and blankets, all perfumed by a Groom with 'swete floures, herbis, roses, and thynges to make them breathe more holesomely and delectable.' Finally, the counterpane laid and cushions arranged, a Squire of the Body blessed the whole bed with holy water. In addition to this daily labour, there were occasional repairs to be made by appointed 'sewers', curtains to be changed, or packed and moved by

41

yeoman hangers, and continual maintenance jobs for other staff. The amount of cleaning required in a sixteenth-century bedroom may be measured by Thomas Tusser's cautionary rhyme:

With curtain some make scabbard clean, with coverlet their shoe:
All dirt and mire, some wallow bed, as spaniels used to do.
The sloven and the careless man, the roynish nothing nice,
To lodge in chamber comely decked, are seldom suffered twice.

The most expensive beds, though often shared with pet dogs, were rarely permitted to suffer the ravages of dust and light. Papers were laid above the canopy, blinds were drawn against the sun, and, when not in use or on view, special case covers were hung from metal rods permanently fixed around the tester.

Smaller eighteenth and nineteenth-century beds, simpler bedding, even fashionable affectations of *déshabillé* did nothing to ease the rituals of bedroom maintenance. More furniture and paraphernalia, and higher standards of cleanliness, spelled-out in scores of housekeeping manuals made the task larger and more exacting. For three generations, from 1860 to 1938, middle-class ladies were led by Mrs. Beeton to order and expect their housemaids to proceed from serving breakfast to emptying bedroom slops, scalding the vessels and removing stubborn stains with turpentine, while the bed, all its clothes removed to 'a horse or the backs of chairs', was aired by the open windows. This done, and the water bottles filled with 'perfectly clean and if possible filtered water', the chambermaid, usually assisted by other servants, could tackle the bed. 'The bed clothes are laid on beginning with an underblanket and sheet, which are tucked under the mattress at the bottom. The bolster is then beaten and shaken and put on, the top sheet rolled round it, and the sheet tucked in all round; the pillows, upper sheet, blankets and bedspread follow, and the eider-down over all. Where spring mattresses are used, care should be taken that the over one is turned every day. The housemaid should now take up any pieces that may be on the carpet or rugs with a sweeper or vacuum-cleaner, dust the room, shut the door, and proceed to another room.' This daily doing was only surface work. Once a week each room was to be 'thoroughly' cleaned–virtually taken apart, shaken, beaten, washed, polished, and restored.

Lucky indeed was the housewife whose expectations of cleanliness were really fulfilled. Jonathan Swift's satirical *Directions to Servants* (an incomplete manuscript written in 1731 and first published in 1925) rings truer, and might have been more useful than the serious sermons delivered by Mrs. Beeton and others. Following Swift's advice, the sensible chambermaid, when she could extract herself from the arms of the footman, would take care never to scour the 'wholesome smell' from the chamber pot, and always to empty it out of the window 'for your lady's credit', to leave the dust in the corner of the room, and to wipe the sweat from her forehead on the corner of the sheet; never to wear a clean apron lest it become rumpled, but always to wear the lady's night dress before it is sent to the laundry; and finally, when the masters are away, to forget all work until the hour before their return.

Bed Warmers: Not only did the bed have to be cleaned and made for the day, it had to be warmed for the night as well. The labour of undoing the clothes, holding them before the fire, and replacing them was considerably lessened in the fifteenth century by long handled warming pans filled with burning embers, and rubbed between the sheets *[figs.26 and 27]*. These brass or silver pans were considered a suitable venue for elaboration often of an erotic nature, referring to bed activities. They are said to have been useful for smuggling in replacements for stillborn noble babies. They were also a common cause of scorched sheets. A box shaped bed-wagon with a charcoal pan suspended within was less risky and less attractive too. A better alternative, infinitely cheaper but not always water-tight, was the stoneware hotwater bottle, known to the French as the *'bassinoire anglaise'*. Multitudes of such flasks (a form which may have suggested to Gladstone the dual purpose bed warmer-tea thermos) were manufactured in assorted sizes and shapes, including the concave belly warmer, and used, often with decorative covers, from the eighteenth to the early twentieth century

Figure 26. Brass Warming Pan, Dutch, dated 1602. Venus and Cupid in the centre.

[fig.28a, b]. Their rubber successors, though not so good for holding drink, have proved more convenient for storage and travel, and remain dependable friends when the central heating and all else fails. They need not even demand a trip to the kitchen to boil the kettle. The 'Supreme Miracle', an extra long immersion heater or, better still, the all-in-one streamline electric bottle could do the boiling on the spot *[fig.28c]*. For all this, the hotwater bottle cannot provide very much more than one square foot of hot bed. The only complete bed

warmers, other than bodies, are electric blankets and electrically heated beds requiring no blankets at all. But, like many luxuries, electricity is a consumer of money, and, more important, of time and thought lest it be a consumer of life as well.

Bed Bugs: A bed, however warm and well made, was no pleasure if one had to share it, as most did, with bed bugs. These blood-sucking insects, the ancient *cimex lectularius*, settled in England sometime in the sixteenth century, and there, protected by the bed curtains, they proliferated. Contemporary sufferers found numerous explanations for the pest. The prime suspect was stale and filthy bedding: heirlooms, according to Thomas Tryon, of 'pernicious Excrements that are breathed forth by the sweating of various sorts of people.' Clean sheets were a good but temporary expedient. Tryon's *Way to Health, Long Life and Happiness,* 1683 was to destroy all stinking feathers and replace them with fresh straw beds in canvas ticks, and flock or wool quilts. Mrs. Thomas Carlyle, driven neurotic by bugs, was frequently tearing down curtains and tossing out infected beds. Others, putting the blame on wood either

Figure 27. Le Coucher, engraving by Sigismund Freudenberger, French, 1775. A *lit à la polonaise* being warmed. Note the bed steps and the *casaquin* nightdress.

45

Figure 28. (a; top left) Stone Hot Water Bottle, *(b; bottom left)* Copper Hot Water Belly Warmer, 19th century, *(c; right)* Electric Hot Water Bottle by Rothermal Ltd., c.1915.

switched to brass beds or to different woods believed to be unsavoury to the bugs. Young Lady Catherine Brydges, granddaughter of the great Duke of Chandos, after one bite, had her cradle lined with slips of bitter wood imported from Jamaica, and was never troubled again. The less extravagant had a wide choice of herbal bags, proprietary bug repellents, and bug traps. Bug-destoying businesses, beginning in the 1730s with the firm of John Southall, did a roaring trade with every rank of society. Tiffin and Son, 'Bug Destroyers to Her Majesty', Princess Charlotte, prospered on the vermin of the upper classes only. Their unparalleled ingenuity was displayed on a large, gas-lit poster celebrating Wellington's destruction of Napoleon: 'MAY THE DESTROYERS OF PEACE BE DESTROYED BY US.'

5 Bedrooms

A special room for a bed to close ones eyes in at night and abandon by day is an extravagant use of space. Thrifty Scots, and others built themselves bed enclosures at one end of the living room. The Japanese have only to slide their walls (paper covered *shiji* or heavier *fusuma*) in grooves to have a bedroom where and whenever they want it. In most civilizations, however, a bedstead merited a room of its own.

Since ancient times it has been customary to sleep upstairs, within reach of wholesome breezes, out of the reach of gnats, dirt and foul odours, away from noisy reception and service rooms. A tower in Egypt, in later times a wing if there was one, or the far ends of the house made the best bed-haven, but not always the most peaceful one. The *enfilade* arrangement of rooms in large sixteenth and seventeenth-century houses made every bedroom save the last a throughway both for people and for winds, like the 'American hurricane' which left Madame de Maintenon virtually paralysed in the King's chamber in Versailles. There were secret passages behind many walls, but as they necessitated more doors they were, in Sir Henry Wotton's opinion, no solution to this 'thing most insufferable.' The Palladian villa arrangement of rooms around a central stair was a solution, particularly appealing to the more intimate life style of the eighteenth century. In most single core houses the principal bedrooms were in the 'attic', the second story above the reception rooms on the first floor or '*piano nobile*'.

The master of a house had to provide sleeping quarters not only for himself, but also for his wife, his children, guests both ordinary and important, and for a hierarchy of attendants and servants permanent and visiting. The larger the house, the greater was the separation of individuals, man and wife, parents and children, and so forth. In a country house the sorting of family, personal attendants (tutors, governesses, body-guards, etc.), and guests was horizontal. In town it was vertical with the wife's room above her husband's. Even on his wedding night Prince Hercule-Mériadec had to climb a secret stair in the Palais Soubise to get from his state bedchamber, specially decorated for the marriage by Boffrand c.1733, to his wife's.

Servants, in town and in the country, were disposed according to rank and rôle, in the basement, the garrets, or over the stables and other service wings. Personal attendants, including concubines and mistresses, stayed closer to their charges. In a royal household they slept virtually everywhere, from the foot of the king's bed in France to the front of the empty throne, respectfully reversed to the wall, in England. Guards dozed before the doors of Odysseus's bedroom; English Gentlemen of the Bedchamber lay in ante-rooms. Thomas, Lord Bruce (later Earl of Ailesbury), attending Charles II, spent an unenviable night sweltering in the heat of a blazing fire, listening to the 'continual chiming' of the King's collection of clocks, and the snuffling of his assorted dogs as they roamed the Apartment.

The bed not only had an assigned room, but a prescribed position within it. Traditionally, a great bed stood projecting into the centre of the room, with only its head against the wall. The French, in the eighteenth century, established a more intimate position, long side to the wall, or better still enclosed in an alcove. Whatever the fashion, it was universally agreed that sleep and expensive textiles were best preserved if the bed did not face the full light of the windows, and if they, in turn, did not face east. Very few people shared Dr. Marie Stopes magnetic sense of north, requiring every bed to be oriented, or certainly slept on in that direction even if this meant lying diagonally or crosswise. (Dickens, Elinor Glyn and Mrs. Gladstone are her only named co-'Magnatates'.)

Never has there been any agreement on the subject of night air, draughts, and ventilation. Draughts were fairly easily avoided by not placing the bed under a window, or in a line between it and the door; by closing the door, and drawing the curtains around the bed and across the windows. The difficulty, however, was letting the 'evil vapours' of sleep out of the room without letting in the equally evil night air. Dr. Edward Borde's answer in 1542 was to shut the windows and keep the fire burning. But the most intense heat could not consume the unpleasant odours of an Elizabethan house. Bedrooms and privy chambers had to be scattered with 'sundry sortes of fragraunte floures' to have the 'comfortable smell' that cheered up the Dutch physician, Levinius Lemnus, visiting England in 1560. Robert Burton, on investigating *The Anatomy of Melancholy* in 1621, found that heat and thirst were the prime causes of insomnia. Unfortunately, he was not so specific in remedying the former as he was the latter. Would he have shared Lord Monboddo's air-baths, or Dr. Stopes pleasure in a 'fine blow when possible'? Lady Barker, author of *The Bedroom and Boudoir*, 1878, would not. Rather than risk the night air, she, like many other hygienic housewives of the nineteenth century, relied on the chimney as a vent, or, failing that, on one of the new patent tubes which could control the flow of air in and out of the room, or into the bed itself.

Double Wicks, in Boxes containing 6 lights and glass (burn 10 hours each). 1s. per Box.

(See figure 36.)

Plate 7. Embroidered Bed Tent. Dodecanese, Cos. c.18th century Detail.

Plate 8 (right). Patchwork Quilt. Pineapple Pattern. American, 2nd half 19th century.

50

Plate 9 (left). Bed and Wash-stand in the Medieval Style. From the Guest Chamber of Tower House, London. Designed by William Burges, 1879.

Plate 10. Cradle of the King of Rome, designed by P.-P. Prud'hon and executed by J. B. C. Odiot and P. P. Thomire, 1811. Engraving from *Modeles de Meubles et de Décorations Interieurs*, Paris, 1841, pl. 69.

Plate 11. Death of Voltaire (d.1778). English painted wax by Samuel Percy (d.1820).

Plate 12 (right). A Night shirt, night cap, and dressing gown belonging to Thomas Coutts, late 19th century, and a lady's pea-green satin lace trimmed-night dress and negligée, and night cap. Early 20th century.

6 Bedroom Furniture

Circuitous Victorian efforts to air the bedroom could not compete with their compulsion to suffocate it with furniture and ornaments. Concern for the day-time entertainment of the houseproud, especially female, or the bed-ridden took precedence over the peaceful sleep of the healthy. In the bedrooms adorned by Lady Barker, every inch of floor space was inhabited by chairs, tables, wash-stands, a 'horse' on which to hang clothes and linen while the bed is being 'made', screens, wardrobes, and chests of drawers *en suite* with the bed, bookcases, and

Figure 29. The Basic Requirements of a Late-19th Century Bedroom before the Addition of a Wealth of Knick-Knacks. Designed in the Japanese style for James Schoolbred and Company, 1876. Published in *Designs of Furniture ... for James Schoolbred and Company, Tottenham House, Tottenham Court Road W.*, 1876, pl.11.

perhaps a piano as well. Each and every object was draped and occupied by brushes, boxes, watch-stands and clocks, vases and bowls, candlesticks and extinguishers. The windows were blocked by frilly dressing tables, cheval mirrors, seats, ferns and aspidistras; there were no flowers in a bedroom. The walls were alive with flowered papers, fans, miniatures, pious and homely pictures, 'pet little odds and ends of china and glass' bestowed on 'diminutive brackets and knobs and hooks.' About night tables beside the bed little was said, but they were an absolute necessity, holding the chamber pot within, and on top a night light, perhaps a simple Clarke's plaster covered 'Burglars Horror', or one of the many ingenious gadgets that gave light, the time, and a warm drink too *[fig.36]*.

'Litter' said Lady Barker, 'is a powerful weapon in the hands of a person who knows how to make a room look comfortable.' It was the standard by which she judged the bedrooms of previous generations. It affords an even better vantage point for us *[fig.29]*.

The cathartic clearance of twentieth-century bedrooms becomes, by comparison, all the more understandable, all the more impressive in its efficiency and clinical tidiness. With everything built into the walls, it is impossible to ask for more space, more hygiene, or less labour. Perhaps it is also impossible, if not ridiculous, to ask for aesthetic pleasures in a room intended for closed eyes. Lifelessness is quintessential to the

Figure 30. Claas Oldenburgh. *The Bedroom*, 1964.

popular image of the 'modern' bedroom. Nowhere is it more potently distilled than in Claas Oldenburg's pop art *Bedroom* of 1964 *[fig.30]*. This life-size environment of a rhomboidal bed with shiny white vinyl sheets, a quilted black plastic bedspread, and ghostly blue and silver dresser, chair and accessories, however nightmarish, is not a dream but a heightened reality, specifically based upon the Las Tunas Motel on the California coast, and typical of the decor depicted in holiday brochures and home-making magazines around the world. Oldenburg's explanation of *Bedroom* is as clear and pertinent as the work itself. 'Geometry, abstraction, rationality . . . are the themes . . . The effect is intensified by choosing the softest room in the house and the least associated with conscious thought . . . /colour/ . . . is limited . . . Hard surfaces and sharp corners predominate. Texture becomes *photographed* texture in the surface of the formica. Nothing 'real' or 'human' . . . The bedroom as rational tomb, pharaoh's or Plato's bedrooms.'

What Victorians might have made of modernity is a matter of speculation. Clearly, they did not regard the bedrooms of their distant ancestors as anything but indecently bare. The grandest

Figure 31. A Night-Table Bason-Stand by Thomas Sheraton, Dated 1793. Published in *The Cabinet-Maker and Upholsterer's Drawing-Book*, Appendix, London, 1794, pl. 7, detail.

seventeenth-century bedchamber contained little more than a Roman *cubiculum*; no more than what was required for the preparation, enjoyment, and conclusion of the passive state of sleep: a bed, steps to mount it, a carpet beside it, a chamber pot, ewer and basin, at least one table on which to rest a candlestick, a chair and perhaps a stool or 'squab', a large chest to store bedlinen and clothes, smaller ones to keep treasured possessions in the safe proximity of their owner. The Middle Ages added an aumbry or livery cupboard to hold the nightly ration of candle wax, bread, wine and ale. Its bedside function is epitomized in the couplet composed by Thomas Tusser in 1573, 'Some slovens from sleeping no sooner be up, but hand is in aumbrie, and nose in the cup.' In the Queen's bedchamber at Whitehall, Pepys noticed nothing but 'some pretty pious pictures, and books of devotion, and her holy water at her head as she sleeps, with a clock by her bed-side, wherein a lamp burns that tells her the time of the night . . . ' Except for the bed, none of the articles found in a bedroom was any different from others of similar type in general use throughout the house. Specific bedroom furniture was a characteristic eighteenth-century rationalisation.

Random Turkey carpets, rush mats and woven ones were marshalled into a distinct and orderly frame, a bed-carpet, around, but not under the bed. Even symbolic state beds that excluded bare feet were well prepared for them. Robert Adam's design for the Osterley bed started at the head and finished on the floor. But only the ancient Persian kings considered human feet second to the feet of the bed for which, according to Xenophon, they provided soft carpets 'in order that the floor might not present resistance to them'.

Chamber pots, having been beautified since Roman times—made of silver inlaid with precious stones, or of earthenware painted with pretty or amusing decorations, were now discreetly secreted in bed steps, pot stands, or night tables conveniently placed alongside the bed *[fig.31]*. Honest close stools were disguised as decorative chairs on which Bourbon kings and others might receive their guests *[fig.32]*.

All bedroom chairs became lighter and more elegant, conforming to the design of the bed. The *chaise longe*, though not new, replaced the chest that traditionally stood at the foot of the bed. The chest, in turn, moved to the wall as a bureau, chest of drawers, or wardrobe. The livery cupboard left for a new place as sideboard in the dining room. Tables began to proliferate with special forms for particular purposes, writing, dressing, washing, etc. For eating in bed there was a tray with folding legs, followed in the early nineteenth century by a pivoting bed-table on an adjustable pillar *[fig.33]*.

The eighteenth century also initiated improvements in the quality and quantity of lighting. Argand's smokeless oil lamp in a glass funnel was invented in 1760, and manufactured in England in the 1780s. Had it been available a decade earlier, it might have prevented the Duke of Bedford's bed at Woburn from becoming 'so very black with the burning of oil'. William Murdock's experiments with coal gas in 1792 brought rosy Victorian gas lights one step closer. Eighteenth-century reason had opened the way for nineteenth-century profusion and twentieth-century purification.

Figure 32 (left). Close stool.
Figure 33. Adjustable chrome and glass bedside table designed by Eileen Grey 1927/28 for a house at Roquebrune.

7 Beds Separate or Shared

Whether one sleeps alone or in company is a matter first of means, and secondly of preference. In a squeeze, virtually any bed can accommodate more than one person at once. The number who could share the nine foot square mattress of the great Bed of Ware, having stretched in its first two hundred years of existence from four couples in 1596 to 'twenty-six butchers and their wives' in 1736, would shrink by present standards to a mere foursome. It was common, until late nineteenth-century health and moral maxims intervened, for children of all classes to sleep together. 'There were ten in a bed, and the little one said, roll over; and they all rolled over, and one fell out.' In Flora Thompson's *Lark Rise to Candleford* it was the eldest who fell out and into work.

Pleasure, usually the prime reason for choosing to share a bed, was not the only one. It was polite sportsmanship that led the Prince de Condé to bed with his defeated opponent, the Duc de Guise, after the battle of Montcour, and sheer necessity that threw Captain Ahab, the hunter of *Moby Dick*, together with the savage Queequag. Married couples, though provided with double beds since Roman times, have not always chosen to keep to them. Those who did so tended to be silent, except for Pepys whose encounters with his volatile wife prove the point of those who, prizing sleep, abandoned and loudly condemned the double bed. The Roman satirist, Juvenal, could find no freedom from 'wrangling and mutual bickering' in a bed that holds a wife; nor could Liselotte, Duchess of Orleans, find freedom of movement in bed with a cantankerous, mysogynist husband who couldn't bear to be touched. Juvenal resorted to boy bed-fellows, and Liselotte to a *lit à part* with her dogs. In the opinion of Dr. Graham, the inventor, in 1743, of The Celestial Bed with 'magnetic effluviums' to 'animate' reproductive powers, the 'most hurtful custom of man and wife continually *pigging* together, in one and the same bed' was 'calculated totally to subvert health, strength, love, esteem . . . everything that is desirable in the married state.' Dr. Stopes fully agreed. To preserve the 'first intensity of love' and a 'truly civilized standard', she would have one bed for one person, and better still separate rooms with a double bed in the wife's room.

The earliest bed expressly intended for one person, the first oval bed too, was Sheraton's design of 1792 for a 'single lady or gentleman.' The true inventor is unknown, but the two large beds in which Charles the Bold of Burgundy and his wife, Isabelle, lay, covered by one vast canopy of green damask and enclosed together by green satin curtains, may be a fifteenth-century forerunner of Robert Adam's abortive design of 1774 for the Earl and Countess of Derby's twin beds under a dome that would have dwarfed the one over the state bed at Osterley, or Sheraton's practical design of 1792 for a 'Summer Bed in two Compartments . . . intended for a nobleman or gentleman and his lady to sleep separately in hot weather' *[fig.34]*. Today, indecisive, lightweight and heavy couples, mis-matches of all kinds are amply provided for with zip together twin-double beds, or, the Swedish ultimate, twin beds separated by a wall which disappears at the press of a button. Despite these ingenious devices for separation, the double bed has not only won the day, it has expanded to king and queen sizes.

Single or otherwise, no clinophile, no pop art dream designer, has yet surpassed the Indian maharajah whose wealth enabled him to enjoy solitude and company, cool breezes and sweet music all at once in a solid silver bed overlooked by four life-size nude female figures painted in realistic colour and detail, fitted with wigs of real hair, and equipped with feathered fans and fly-whisks. He had merely to lie down for the music and fanning automatically to commence *[fig.35]*. All that he lacked was Alan Jones's table (1967), supported by a woman on all fours wearing nothing but black gloves and high-heeled boots, on which to rest his night-light.

Figure 34 (left).
'A Summer Bed in Two Compartments' by Thomas Sheraton, dated 1792. Published in *The Cabinet-Maker and Upholsterer's Drawing-Book, Part III*, London, 1794, pl. 41.

Figure 35. A solid silver bed made for an Indian Maharajah.

8 Dressing for Bed

Since ancient times it has been commonplace to sleep clothed. Only in the Middle Ages, from the eleventh to the fifteenth century, was nudity the rule, and it was a rule included, for example, in a thirteenth-century marriage contract that a wife should not sleep in a chemise without her husband's consent. Child-birth, illness, a ceremonial visit, a deformity needing disguise, or a wish to resist love-making were among the few occasions on which night dress might be worn. The medieval insistence on nudity in bed has been related to their total distinction between the sexes in all other aspects of life, that would have been contradicted by clothing men and women in identical sleeping garments. Hence, instead of inventing pyjamas for men, they dispensed with clothes altogether.

Why most other civilized people sleep clothed is not so easy to explain. Is it the result of greater equality between the sexes, or, as Dr. Stopes maintained, simply because 'when the healthy habit of one person one bed is adopted, the personal heat is not always enough to warm the bed quickly enough for sleep'?

Before the mid-nineteenth century most sleeping garments were either underwear or something not much different, shirts or chemises. (The term 'night' prefixed to an article of clothing distinguished indoor from outdoor wear, not sleep wear.) Romans, forbidden to wear a toga while lying on the bed alive, slept in a tunic, their main undergarment. Ladies of that period kept on a bra, loin cloth, and possibly a mantle as well, but removed a wealth of make-up, intricate hair-pieces and jewellery, and lay, as Martial said, 'stored away in a hundred caskets.' After an absence of four hundred years, night clothes returned in the sixteenth century virtually unaltered–simple, hand-made tunics with more or less decoration to distinguish the sex and wealth of the wearer.

For men, it was the night shirt *[pl.12]* or nothing until the end of the nineteenth century, when two piece pyjamas were introduced. This was often the gayest garment they had. It was also, in Dr. Stopes's view, the most uncomfortable, with its strangling cord, its parting waist, popping buttons, and legs that ruck up. On the basis of personal experience, she recommended boys' all-in-one combinations 'made and properly cut for grown-up men by tailors'.

The history of ladies' nightwear up to the mid-nineteenth century is not much different from men's. Except for the eighteenth-century French casaquin, a highly seductive night-dress, low-necked and tight-waisted. There were only minor variations upon the shapeless, covered-up chemise. With the advent of competitive commercialism, nightwear was at last able, indeed required, to keep pace with changing fashions in other dress. Like underwear, it became more and more feminine, flimsy, revealing and appealing. That this trend was concurrent with the removal of bed curtains and the introduction of birth control in the 1880s may not be mere coincidence. Prim or alluring, the nightgowns worn by our grandmothers are now appreciated as fashionable day and evening wear.

The past hundred years have witnessed high-waisted Empire styles alternating with fully gathered and slinky, bias-cut dresses, thin shoulder straps and billowing bishops' sleeves, high necks, plunging backs, and various shapes and degrees of décolletage. Skirts, at first, were lengthened to reach the floor. Having come down, they then went up and up, eventually reaching the hip-length 'baby doll' dress for which panties were provided. Traditional fine cotton, and wool for winter were joined by a host of other fabrics: satin, artificial washing silk, nuns' veiling, voile, lawn, transparent lace and chiffon, and recently nylon and other synthetics. There was a profusion of trimmings too: ruffles, pleats, tucks, embroidery, ecru lace, and a peculiar taste for pink baby ribbon. White, having been the most common colour for nearly two thousand years, ceased to be fashionable, and was relegated mainly to less well-off ladies, and to brides. The English bride of 1903 was advised to equip her trousseau with at least two dozen nightdresses, preferably of 'the purest white', definitely not of 'black silk or gauze' favoured by 'Americans and other ultra-smart folk'. The discreet pastel shades that were popular in the late nineteenth century gave way in the 1920s and 30s to Hollywood shades: Madonna blue, tulip leaf green, turquoise, melon, rose and so forth *[pl.12]*. The contemporary craze for pyjamas was no less romantic. Made to comply with boyish whims or exotic harem affectations, they were worn night and day for sleeping and lounging.

Regardless of what, if anything, was worn on the body, a covering for the head was *de rigueur* for everyone from the Middle Ages to the end of the nineteenth century. Most people had white or red nightcaps for normal use, black ones for mourning; linen for summer wear, quilted cotton, wool or flannel for winter. Knitted or crotcheted 'network' caps were considered unfashionable until nineteenth-century hygienists, like Dr. Robert Macnish, declared ventilation to be more important than warmth and beauty. No one challenged silk as the highest and most desirable luxury. Most men were content just to pull on a simple jelly bag, a turban, or a tasselled stocking-cap. William Vaughan, in 1602, thought it imperative to have a hole in the top 'through which the vapours may goe out'; others required strings or buttons under the chin to keep the cap on, vapours and all. Mr. Pickwick, his 'confounded strings in a knot', had to suffer the overwhelming embarrassment of being seen in his nightcap by the middle-aged lady who happened to be occupying the bed next to his at the inn.

Such tragedies rarely befell the ladies. Their nightcaps, or 'night coifs', sometimes worn with 'night cross-cloths' across the forehead, were far more attractive than their chemises; in many cases attractive enough to be seen in around the house as well as in bed. Fashions, however extreme, always guaranteed undisturbed hair. Undisturbed sleep was quite beside the point.

9 Getting Up

The inevitable conclusion of going to bed is getting up, an unpleasant business of questionable virtue for many, an essential one for most of us. 'To be alive', in ancient or modern Rome, is 'to be awake', as Pliny said; early enough to capture the coolness of the morning before being forced to return to bed by the heat of the mid-day sun. Dr. Johnson, Jonathan Swift, Joseph Addison, G. K. Chesterton, and other northerners were no less healthy, wealthy, and wise for being late to bed and late to rise. The majority, however, are not so fortunate as to have a job and a conscience that totally agrees with their pleasures and inclinations. A bedside aid is required to settle the disagreement for them.

Uncompromising portable alarm clocks began ringing in the early fifteenth century, when the spring drive replaced the weight. They were followed in the next and later centuries by all sorts of ingenious devices to cushion the discomforts of leaving the bed. An alarm clock that lit a candle was invented in 1500, and improved many times over until the electric switch appeared at the end of the nineteenth century. The '*veilleuse*', a combination alarm clock, night light and food warmer, produced in 1762 by M. Musy of Paris, went through several nineteenth-century variations before it emerged as a modern 'Teasmade' *[figs.36, 37, 38]*. For all this, there was still no surety that sluggards behind the bed curtains would hear the bells and see the lights, let alone heed them. M. Morgues of Marseilles attempted to solve the problem in 1781 with a gadget that rang, lit a candle, drew the bed curtains and opened the window. Eviction was finally achieved, and displayed in the Crystal Palace, in 1851 by R. W. Savage's 'Alarum Bedstead' that removed the bed clothes and tilted sideways depositing its occupant on the floor.

CLARKE'S "PYRAMID" NURSERY
LAMP FOOD WARMER.

2s. 6d., 3s. 6d., 5s., and 6s. each.

Figure 36. Clarke's Night-light Food-Warmer. Advertisement, *Illustrated London News*, 26 Nov. 1892.

Figure 37 (above right). An Automatic Tea-making Machine with Alarm Clock, c.1904.

Figure 38 (below right). The Goblin 'Teasmade', 1977.

Dr. Stopes would have none of the gadgets adored by her Victorian ancestors. Anyone who needs an alarm clock, needs more sleep. Should a clock be considered essential, she wrote, it must be one that does not rush or waken, but lulls you to sleep, like the muffled tick of a watch in a tufted watch-pocket pinned to the head board as it had been for centuries, a chimeless grandfather clock, or any other provided its tick is proven, tested in the shop, to be the same or slower than your own heart beat.

Men and women have certainly made going to bed a complex affair. Perhaps, after reading the history of this universal custom, looking at depictions and relics of past beds, we will be more grateful for what little is left of the bed now, and enjoy it before some scientific substitute for sleep terminates its future forever.

Bibliography

The following list includes only those sources that have been used or quoted in the text. It does not include all histories of furniture and decoration in which beds are discussed. Bibliographies for further study are noted in the works listed here. Page references have been given for quotations taken from lengthy books, in which they might otherwise be difficult to locate.

Aslin, E., *Nineteenth Century English Furniture*, 1962. (bibl.)

Ayres, J. E., 'American Coverlets', *Textile History*, I, 1, 1968.

Baker, Hollis S., *Furniture in the Ancient World*, 1966.

Barker, Lady (Broome, M. A.), *The Bedroom and Boudoir*, 1878

Beeton, I. M., *Household Management*, (n. d.)

Boynton, L. O. J., 'The Bed-Bug And The 'Age of Elegance'', *Furniture History*, I, 1963, pp. 13–31; (bibl.)

British Museum, *Treasures of Tutankhamun*, 1972, nos. 13. 37.

Carcopino, J., *Daily Life in Ancient Rome*, 1970.

Cardigan, The Earl of, *The Life and Loyalties of Thomas Bruce*, 1951, pp. 78–80.

Cunnington, C. W. and P., *The History of Underclothes*, 1951.

De la Mare, W., *Behold, This Dreamer*, 1939, pp. 191–192.

Ecke, G., *Chinese Domestic Furniture*, 1963.

Eden, M. and Carrington, R., *The Philosophy of the Bed*, 1961, (bibl.)

Edis, R. W., *Decoration and Furniture of Town Houses*, 1889, p. 220.

Evelyn, J., *The Diary of John Evelyn*, ed. E. S. de Beer., 1959, pp. 151, 239, 242, 387.

Fowler, J. and Cornforth, J., *English Decoration in the 18th Century*, 1974.

Gallet, M. (tr. J. C. Palmes), *Paris Domestic Architecture of the 18th Century*, 1972.

Giedion, S., *Mechanization Takes Command*, 1948, pp. 431–435.

Gray, C. and M., *The Bed*, 1946.

Harris, E., *Furniture of Robert Adam*, 1973.

Havard, H., *Dictionnaire de l'Ameublement et de la Décoration depuis le XIIIe siècle jusqu'à nos jours*, 1887–09, III.

Hayward, H. ed., *World Furniture*, 1970. (bibl.)

Hughes, T., 'Old English Quilting', *Country Life Annual*, 1956, pp. 108–171.

Hunt, L., 'Beds and Bedrooms', *Men, Women and Books*, I, 1847, pp. 114–128.

Jackson-Stops, G., 'William III and French Furniture', *Furniture History*, VII, 1971, pp. 121–126.

Johnstone, P., *A Guide to Greek Island Embroidery*, 1972.

Kates, G., *Chinese Household Furniture*, 1962.

Kroll, M. (tr. and ed.), *Letters from Liselotte*, 1970, pp. 83, 98–99, 113.

Liversidge, J., *Furniture in Roman Britain*, 1955.

MacQuoid, P. and Edwards, C. H. R., *Dictionary of English Furniture*, 1954. (beds, cradles, night tables)

Meade, D., *Bedrooms*, Design Centre, 1967.

Murray Baillie, H., 'Etiquette and the Planning of the State Apartments in Baroque Palaces', *Archaeologia*, CI, 1967, pp. 169–199.

O'Dea, W. T., *The Social History of Lighting*, 1958.

Paine, R. T., 'Chinese Ceramic Pillows from Collections in Boston and Vicinity', *Far Eastern Ceramic Bulletin*, VII, 3, Sept. 1955.

Pevsner, N., *Pioneers of Modern Design*, 1960, p. 154.

Ransom, C. L., *Couches and Beds of The Greeks, Etruscans and Romans*, 1905.

Richter, G., *Handbook of Greek Art*, 1974.

Russel, J. and Gublik, S., *Pop Art Redefined*, 1969, pp. 95–96.

Safford, C. L. and Bishop, R., *America's Quilts and Coverlets*, 1972.

Saint-Laurent, C., *A History of Ladies Underwear*, 1968, chap.4.

Stopes, M. C., *Sleep*, 1956.

Swift, J., *Directions to Servants*, 1925.

Symonds, R. W., 'The Bed Through The Centuries', *The Connoisseur*, CXL, Jan.–June 1943, pp. 34–43.

Thornton, P., 'French Beds', *Apollo*, March 1974, pp. 182–185.

Thornton, P., 'Two Problems', *Furniture History*, VII, 1971.

Ward-Jackson, P., *English Furniture Designs of the 18th Century*, 1958.

Wardle, P., *Guide to English Embroidery*, 1970.

Whitfield, R., 'Tz'u-chou Pillows with Painted Decoration', *Chinese Painting and The Decorative Style. Colloquies on Art and Archaeology in Asia*, no. 5, p. 80.

Wotton, H., *The Elements of Architecture*, 1624, p. 72.

Wright, L., *Warm and Snug, The History of the Bed*, 1962. (bibl.)

Index

Adam, Robert 22, 26, 59, 62
Alarm clocks 67–9
Bed 5, 11
  alcove 27
  ancient 11
  camp 14–15
  cupboard 14, 34
  death 39–40, 54
  double 61–2
  feather 5–6, 45
  four-poster 17, 27, 31
  French 15, 16, 23
  hundred years, in the last 30–4
  marriage 10, 29, 36
  medieval style 52
  metal 30–2, 35, 46
  mourning 39
  parlour 34
  price of 13
  silver 62–3
  single 62
  sofa 34, 35
  state 17, 22, 24–6, 39, 41–2
  truckle 14
  twin 62, 63
  Ware, great bed of 16–17, 61
  18th and 19th century 26–30, 42
Bed bugs 30, 45–6
Bed chamber 17, 24–6, 41–2, 59
Bed covers 6, 13, 29, 30, 41–2
Bed curtains 15, 27, 31–2, 33, 38,
    41, 65
Bed hangings 12, 22, 27–30
Bed making 41–2
Bed Warmers 14, 43–5

Bedroom 28, 30, 47–9, 56–60
Bedroom furniture 23, 32, 33, 34,
    39, 56–60
Bedroom ventilation 31–2, 48–9, 56
Bedstead 5, 8–10, 12, 27, 33
Birth 36–7
Blankets 6
Canopy 11, 12, 14, 27, 38, 42, 62
Chamber pot 14, 42, 57, 59
China 7, 8, 10
Cleaning beds and bedrooms 41–3
Couch 9–10, 16
Cradle 19, 32, 37–9, 46, 53
Egyptians 7, 8, 9, 11, 47
Foot Board 8, 27
Greeks 5, 6, 7, 9, 29
Head board 27, 33
Head rest 7
Industrial Revolution 30–1
Japan 5, 8, 41, 47
Kline 9, 10, 34
Mattress 5–6, 33, 42
Middle ages 8, 41, 59, 64
Middle ages to 18th century 12–24
Nightwear 55, 64–6
Pillows 7
Quilts 6, 29, 36, 51
Renaissance 7, 12, 17, 31
Romans 5, 6, 9, 10, 30, 41, 61, 64
Sheets 6–7
Sheraton, Thomas 15, 35, 37, 62, 63
Stopes, Marie 6, 7, 48, 49, 62, 64,
    68
Tester 14–15, 19, 27, 38, 42
Victoria and Albert Museum 12–13

Printed in England for Her Majesty's Stationery Office by Balding + Mansell, Wisbech
Dd. 587516 K80